Ancient Acid Flashes Back

T0097597

Western Literature Series

Books by Adrian C. Louis

POETRY

Muted War Drums (Chapbook, 1977)

Sweets for the Dancing Bears (Chapbook, 1979)

Fire Water World (1989)

Among the Dog Eaters (1992)

Days of Obsidian, Days of Grace (1994)

Blood Thirsty Savages (1994)

Vortex of Indian Fevers (1995)

Ceremonies of the Damned (1997)

Skull Dance (Chapbook, 1998)

Ancient Acid Flashes Back (2000)

FICTION

Skins (1995)

Wild Indians & Other Creatures (1996)

ADRIAN C. LOUIS

Ancient Acid
POEMS Flashes Back

University of Nevada Press ▲▲ Reno & Las Vegas

Western Literature Series

University of Nevada Press, Reno, Nevada 89557 USA

Copyright © 1979, 1993, 1994, 1995, 1996, 1997,
1998, 2000 by Adrian C. Louis

Library of Congress Cataloging-in-Publication
Louis, Adrian C.
Ancient acid flashes back : poems / Adrian C. Louis.
p.   cm. — (Western literature series)
ISBN 0-87417-352-3 (alk. paper)
1. Paiute Indians—Poetry.   2. Indians of North
America—Poetry.   3. Haight-Ashbury (San
Francisco, Calif.)—Poetry.   I. Title.   II. Series.
PS3562.082 A84   2000
811'.54—dc21   00-008552

FIRST PRINTING
09 08 07 06 05 04 03 02 01 00
5 4 3 2 1

For Colleen with love.

For those who were there.

The great epochs of our life are the occasions
when we gain the courage to rebaptize our
evil qualities as our best qualities.

—FRIEDRICH NIETZSCHE

Here are the years that walk
between, bearing away the fiddles
and the flutes, restoring one who moves
in time between sleep and waking . . .

—T. S. ELIOT

Contents

Acknowledgments

Some of the poems included in this volume have been pub-
lished previously, many in earlier versions, in *TriQuarterly,
The Pittsburgh Quarterly, Exquisite Corpse, Spike, Atom Mind,
Chiron Review, The Hungry Mind Review, Hawaii Pacific Re-
view, Long Shot, Zen Tattoo, Cedar Hill Review, Poetry Motel,*
and in *Days of Obsidian, Days of Grace* (Poetry Harbor Press,
1994). Several of these poems also appeared in the chapbook
Sweets for the Dancing Bears (Blue Cloud Abbey Press, 1979)
and in the anthology *Thus Spake the Corpse* (Black Sparrow
Press, 1999).

The author extends thanks to Keith Abbott, Greg Smith,
and Trudy McMurrin for offering suggestions on the vari-
ous incarnations of the manuscript. Thanks also to Mar-
garet, Carrie, and the rest of the crew at the University of
Nevada Press. Finally, I am indebted to Bill Holm for meals,
lodging, conversation, and employment. I bow down be-
fore his huge and generous Icelandic heart.

Ancient Acid Flashes Back

A Prayer Opens the Floodgates

It's the nipping dog of prairie heat
that breeds invocation. June '99 &
Naatsi is middle-aging gracelessly
smackdab in the middle of America.
Surrendering to his sputtering
lawnmower on a blistering Dakota day,
he retreats indoors to soothe his high
blood pressure & smoke one of his
daily ration of ten cigarettes.

Sitting, still sweating, deep-breathing,
he watches some rednecks on ESPN
careening their stock cars
in the Winston Cup Series.
He has little choice—the remote
control is out of reach, hiding out
upon the farthest realms
of the scarred coffee table.
These race cars are plastered
with advertising & he's wishing
all the bastards would crash
& then he prays:

O Grandfather, please take the
grandstands of drunken crackers
& transport them to the Gobi Desert
& match them up against
a phalanx of Compton Crips.

Let 'em have a hillbilly
& gangsta hoedown!
Yes, Lord, make them dance,
please make them smooch
like long-lost, lonely brothers . . .

& O Holy Jesus, do something
about those cars, whoa,
they're all painted loco!
That one's a big jug
of Tide Detergent,
& this other mother's a huge
box of Kellogg's Corn Flakes
& Christ, they're torquing
my brain back to Haight
Street, the 60's where
photon torpedoes
of acid exploded
my eyeballs,
my soul &
my groin.

The Boy Hears Distant Drums
From Across the Sierras

Yerington, Nevada. July '66
& *Naatsi* is newly nineteen,
laboring for Anaconda Copper
Mine, guiding house-sized
Dart dump trucks along
a dirt road to belch
their loads at an ore crusher
or pour the leached rock
over the tailings slopes
& once or twice a shift
giving the drivers a break,
taking their trucks up
from the ancient depths, up
the inclines of the pit mine
(sixth largest in the world!)
& he thinks he's got it made,
sunshine, company bunk, commissary
credit, & plenty of cash, enough
left over come Friday night
for the cathouse ladies
to do him real nice.

He watches the line of yellow
dump trucks parade upon
the earth like a shimmering
herd of fallen chunks of sun.
They puke green rock
into the ore crusher until

the noon air whistle
screams a bolt of calm
that rips open thermoses
& steel lunchbuckets.

Finished with his Spam
sandwiches & Kool-Aid,
Naatsi ambles away
from the sun.
The dust devils pester
like the nagging, dry wives
the older miners complain of
& he searches for shade
to become brothers
with lizards: lean & cosmic,
dozing & silent & in
the queer desert quiet
he hears distant drums
from across the Sierras.
They call him to leave
his home spirit-soil
& join up with renegade
seekers of freedom
& other enemies
of the state.

Bad Orange Sunshine Flashback

SAN FRANCISCO! Late August,
late 60's & *Naatsi* purposely
passed gas & walked out of the office
because the shrink had skunk
breath & said something
immensely intelligent like
"If you objectify your plight
with the fatal interrogatives
then healing catharsis will occur."

He sucked down a small roach
& hiked back up to the Haight
where he crashed with Noreen,
an *artiste* who made boobs
out of plaster of Paris.
When they dried, she spraypainted
them with red or green or blue
metal-flake paint & glued
a cat's-eye marble where
each nipple should be.

Noreen's the one who
made him shave the hairs
around the shaft of his war lance.
She said it made him slick,
all the more handsome.
Oh, he was young & knew
very little of split-tail ways.

Over the Sierras in the dry Indian
time warp he'd come from,
white boys were still running
the single wing & his mom
& his brutal white stepfather were
endlessly staggering in desert heat.

Noreen was the first white woman he'd ever
had so he promised her he'd see
a shrink after he freaked
on a tab & a half of bad
orange sunshine one night
& shot-putted twenty of her titties
out the window onto Oak Street
where they exploded like milk
grenades on black asphalt.
"Far out, but either get some
counseling," she said the next
morning—"Or split."

Well, he lasted five more weeks
with her in tit heaven
but he never went back
to that shrink with skunk breath
& maybe blew the chance to nip
decades of angry-dick madness
then & there in the bud.

On Love Street

O sweet generosity of human mindflesh.
On Love Street . . . where life tasted good,
Naatsi was released from the arrogant
white bread stupidity of ORDER
& the beachboy–hotrod–jockstrap
emulation of his high school days,
so he grew hair longer than any Indian
he'd ever seen outside the silver screen.

O sweet generosity of human mindflesh.
Zap Comix & smoke released him
from the ghastly primer
of the Texas Schoolbook Depository
so he balled his brains out
& truly believed days
of dope & no money
were preferable to days
of money & no dope.

O sweet generosity of human mindflesh.
On Love Street . . . where life tasted good
& he became invisible to America
& America became invisible to him,
he released himself from the crotch-rot
demands of jungled Vietnam.
By smoking weed he thought
he could discern the goofy face
of God in the mirror.

God was there & God
you know was good . . .

Now, three decades later,
he wonders if he was poisoned
when he inhaled the last gasps
of freedom in those lush days
before the mind control
machines in the living
rooms of America
possessed our souls.

Love Street, where did you go?
Now he's gray & incomplete
& afraid most of the time.
There's not a single acre of soil
in America where it's safe to live.
Naatsi can't remember the last time
his groin got hard of its own accord,
but yes, oh *yes,* the fool still has
jasmine-scented dreams of a
much sweeter & somehow
a wiser, yet truly more
innocent time.

Reductio Ad Absurdum

How art thou fallen from heaven,
O Lucifer, son of the morning.
—ISAIAH 14:12–14

Like the singer said,
the times were a'changing.
In '67 the loony moon ripened.
It exploded & rained down
upon San Francisco, covering
The City with green voodoo cheese.
Off & on for several years, *Naatsi*
walked without underwear among
the crazy white Indians who told his
desert brain why America had failed.
Wearing beads & blowing weed,
they spoke through their beards:

Obviously, man . . . check it out.
The very foundation
of this nation is weak.
Look around you.
In the eternal anger
of the slums, the dark
ones like the Mexicans
& the African sons
of slaves are refusing
to play the game for 'the man.'
Why should they pull themselves up
by their own bootstraps anymore?
Amerika *was doomed from the start.*
It's karma. It's because of what

9

we did to the Indians!
It's because of what we're
still doing to the Indians!
Damn, you should know that.
You really should know that.
Listen . . . !
You do know that,
don't you, brother?

Puzzled, he shook his head firmly
first yes, then no, then yes again.
He smiled & asked for
more mighty Michoacán.
On the side, he was still looking
for backbreaking bullwork
to sweat-sprout the seeds
of the white demon dreams
though he no longer sought
a magic back door
to sneak into Rockwell's
fluffy *Post* portraits.

A Few Indians Are Around

This new world he's landed
on truly mystifies *Naatsi.*
A few Indians are around, but
it's mostly swarms of white folk
dressed in carnival threads
& they're fed up with *Amerika*
yet at the same time they're
deathly afraid of *Amerika.*

They're more like mixed-up kids
than enemies of the state.
They dance down city streets
& scatter marijuana seeds
in the sidewalk cracks.
That's okay with him.
He's just a *nomogwet,*
a *taibo naatsi,* a half-breed
with a volcano in his pants
& the girls here love lava.
He loves this place
of milk & honey, this big
rock & roll candy mountain.

Yeah, he says he don't expect
to live past thirty & man . . .
thirty's light-years away.
Maybe he's just prolonging
childhood. Maybe he's

just too impressionable in
the wrong time in history.
The more stoned he gets,
the less he worries.

A few Indians are around, but
it's mostly swarms of white people
& they've had it with *Amerika*.
Lots of them walking around
with bells tied to their clothes
& flowers in their hair.
Every place he walks into
there's a god's eye made of yarn
& a pot of stale brown rice
on the stove & pot smoke
dancing in the air.
He really likes these people!
They say anyone past thirty
is the enemy, don't trust them.
Dig it, *Naatsi* don't
expect to live
past thirty & man . . .
thirty's light-years away.

Light-years away.

Love Strikes

In Golden Gate Park
beneath Hippie Hill
near the benches
filled with conga players
Naatsi saw her electric
thighs shimmering, sweating,
perfectly thumping
to heart sounds amplified
by wine & weed.
There was nothing else
to do but shake his
half-breed butt alongside her.
He did an awkward reflection
of her demon dance
& later she let him buy
her some fish & chips.
Said her name was Maya Wu.
Said she'd ball him for a lid,
then said she was just kidding.
She'd ball him for free.
That's what she said.
That's what she did.

Maya Wu's Eyes

Fine long black hair
& smooth tan skin.
Could have been Indian
except for those eyes.
Eyes that flayed him.
Eyes that x-rayed him.
Eyes that loved him
& eventually betrayed him.
Could have been Indian
except for those eyes.

Head Lines

His balls were flopping free
inside his Navy surplus bell bottoms.
He was starting to peak on acid on Market
Street his first month in The City
when his black & white thoughts
transformed to Technicolor
like Dorothy leaving Kansas.
Naatsi came upon a tourist register
book in front of a jewelry store
& flipping through the pages
saw the names of two Indian cats
from his home soil & knew
they were probably at Fort Ord
building muscles so they could
go & kill the commie gooks.
He signed his name & after
it he wrote his hometown
& then in parentheses
(WAR KILLS!)
followed by the peace sign.
O young puppy dog that he was,
so naive & so blissfully unaware
then that the true religion
of man is killing his fellow man.

Aquarius

His street brother Doyle
was an Aquarius who looked
like Errol Flynn & knew it.
Doyle often told *Naatsi*
"There is so little left to know
when you realize the known
world exists below—our belts."
Women swarmed around Doyle
& he was generous with them.
He grabbed them two at a time.
When their lonely hobo hell
was fired by flaming groins,
Doyle would say, "Heads or tails,"
& *Naatsi* felt the drugged-out
bliss of spinning—a coin tossed
up into winds of warm
woman freakflesh.

Panhandlers' Picnic

It was all there for the asking.
Doyle & *Naatsi* panhandled
for twenty minutes & scrounged
up forty-five clams from tourists
who thronged to the human zoo
to throw their spare change at freaks.
They scored a matchbox of gold,
some strawberry rolling papers,
a gallon of burgundy,
a large order of fish & chips,
a pack of Kools, a pack of Marlboros,
two barbecued fried bologna sandwiches,
ten pirogis from the Ukrainian bakery
& some spearmint gum
& then they trucked down
to Golden Gate Park
to trade all their supplies
for some sleek pelts of beaver.

Desperate Days

Winter rain.
No tourists, no gain.
Saint Anthony's beans for lunch.
For dessert, a roach stuck
between two matches is ignited
for a few seconds of happy pain.

The next day up in North Beach
down on Broadway past the barkers
into the darkness with enough money
for two drinks, Doyle & *Naatsi*
chortled at Carol Doda & her mind
blowing tits & then went
looking for a pawn shop
to hock their high school rings
so they could score
the milk-blood
of bliss & pretend
they knew freedom.

Brautigan: 1967

Brautigan was looking
so safely bohemian
with a floppy gray fedora
& flaxen hair dangling
onto his new pea coat.
The cat was sipping steam
beer at the MDR on Grant.
Naatsi smiled & said, "Cool"
when his pal Doyle, who
was zippered into goofiness
on reds & short dogs of tokay,
told Brautigan: "Say us a poem."
Naatsi giggled, thinking probably
Brautigan was plastic & perhaps
really straight, but then (epiphany!)
he felt embarrassed & walked away
because his paws hadn't clutched a pen
& he had no poems to show but the holes
in his soles which were covered
with cardboard to hold
in the stink.

Kaufman: 1968

In an alley off Grant
Maya & *Naatsi* tripped
upon poor Bob Kaufman
that old Beat poet who wrote
about golden sardines & such
& was dog-howling at the neon,
perhaps, or shrieking at invisible
light bulbs dancing upon his tongue.
They stopped & passed him a lit doobie
& Kaufman mumbled something at them
& smiled when he passed it back.
They toked from a distance
never touching their lips
to where madness had
kissed deeper
madness.

Naatsi gave the eerie poet
the roach & floated off with Maya
to Chinatown to buy her
fried shrimp & the white
rice of her race.

Speed Freaks on Stanyan

Is there no balm in Gilead?
Is there no physician here?
—JEREMIAH 8:18–9:1

Bumstinking unwashed
& red-eyed unholy,
the Nevada boy was beyond
desperate when he crashed
with some speed freaks
in their crab-infested
Stanyan Street pad.
These wired crankheads
were downright spooky
& some had guns, but all
had typewriter teeth &
non-stop nouns & verbs.

In the tense darkness,
he watched their half
moon eyeballs flit
from wall to wall
& bounce eerily off
blacklight posters.
Their short, hard lives
were closing in on them.
They tied off with belts,
shot up & peeked
out grimy windows
& waited all night
for American KGB
devils to burst in

& slather their groins
with molasses & fire ants.

When the morning sun
spoked rays through
their India print curtains,
they jitter-jived & moaned
like trapped vampires.
An ambulance screamed
up the sunny street
& pure fear sweated
out all their meth.
When he saw them
fixing up for breakfast,
he threw his toothbrush
into his backpack
& escaped to the park
where he hunkered under
a eucalyptus tree
& prayed for them,
for all the lost souls,
yes, he did, Lord,
yes, he did, damn you, Jesus,
you hairy-assed hippie
of biblical strut.

Dark Circle

Walking toward the park
in the green morning mist
Doyle said the raw-brained
white chicks from farms
& suburbs were easy
pickings for Fillmore pimps.
Said, "Watch them spades—
they'll rip you off."

Doyle was from South
Boston & had no damn
use for black people at all.
Called them inventive names
& always clocked them out
of the corner of his eye.

Blacks were new to *Naatsi*.
He'd never seen any at home
so he adopted the white man's
eyeball of fear & contempt
for a while & it took him some
time to see he was looking
down on the blacks the same
way the white man did
his people back home
in redneck Nevada.

Sharon, a Pretty Blond Cheerleader

One day during his first months in Oz
he runs into Sharon, a pretty blond
cheerleader he went to school with.
She's selling lids on the street, dressed in
raggedy-ass clothes & he's shocked, shocked
that she runs up to him & gives him a
big wet kiss on the lips. Sharon never
really spoke to him in high school, ran
with the rich white crowd & never
said much except the occasional hi.
Right on the street she fires up a joint
of killer weed & they get blitzed, the
next thing he knows he's on a bus
with her heading for Potrero Hill
& she's saying how she'd really
like to ball Jim Morrison &
so he asks her if she'd like to ball
& she says no & he says why
& she says you know & he says no,
how come & she's so fucking stoned
she says because *you're* Indian
& he hops off the bus somewhere
in the Mission District & he wonders
how home followed him here.

At the Coffee Gallery

Psychedelic riffs
of stoned haze
from the jukebox
crawled up to his ears
& down to his penis
which was scheming how
to lasso some dog-faced dog
who'd only merit doggie-style
when Janis Joplin walked in
with a chick named Sunshine
& sat on a stool next to HIM.
He was down to his last
dollar & couldn't even offer
to buy her a drink, so he
melted down to the floor
& oozed out the door.
Went to a public toilet
& pounded his pride.
Damn, she was fine.
Damn, he was good!
Strong wood and batting
a thousand in fantasyland.

She Speaks, He Listens

Raving, coming down hard,
Maya Wu said the great
lies of television, those aberrations
& perversions of American life,
jizzed through the air & cloaked
the citizens with a quilt of confusion.
Coming down hard, she said in the real
air of his arid homeland, the eagle
still screamed & sometimes now
Naatsi could barely hear it.
Go home to your people, she said.
You stay here, you'll die, she screeched
& then said he was too hypnotized
by Walter Cronkite & the insect
jaws of Walt Disney.
Coming down, she told him
he had forgotten almost everything
that is good. Be a coyote, she said.
Then she borrowed twenty bucks
& floated toward Love Street
to find her connection.

Listening to The Doors

Listening to The Doors, radio blasting
& toking mind-bending hash & speeding
from Berkeley toward The City in Maya's
parents' paneled Ford wagon, he tripped
on the colony of driftwood sculptures
in the mud flats before the Bay Bridge.
The hash, the car, Jim Morrison & the eerie
sculptures pushed him toward panic.
Naatsi prayed for calm & reached
out to the small town of his desert mind.
He remembered always watching the pimpled
white kids leave his high school at three
& spin their parents' cars out of the parking
lot as disturbed as a nest of angry bees
searching for an invisible honey thief.

The Indian kids, too poor to own cars,
placed their feet upon the earth
& moped toward their future
or was it their past? They weren't
dreaming of Wovoka or Crazy Horse.
They were dreaming of a good used car
like Maya's parents' paneled Ford wagon.

Higher Than Holy Rollers

Light blesses the freaks in the park.
Unconditional Father Sun anoints
their heads with delirious sweat.
A wind whips a thousand heartbeats
into a low, loving murmur.
In the sweet illusion of feathers
& glass beads & buckskin,
Naatsi's half-red whirlwinds
of regret disappear.
For this instant in eternity,
the entire spinning earth
is all young & smiling.
The whole world has lost winter.
It is the Summer of Love
& the people are dancing.
Life is beautiful & people are dancing.
Sweat-popping crazy under the sun,
they smile like coyotes, higher
than holy rollers & low like
the sad funk of sweet delta blues.

Peyote Dream

He dreams he's floating
above the spinning earth. Below,
in the middle of dry Paiute country,
inside a squat, whitewashed shack shooting
woodsmoke at the stars is the woman he loves.
She knows little of the white man ways.
She's a good cook. She loves to cook.
She knows so little of the white man ways.
She's a good mother. Loves all kids.
She's his buckskin brownskin dreamwife.
She wipes his tears when he cries.
She laughs when he cries. Yes,
she laughs when he cries.
She's so strong & so far away.
The spirits of peyote bind her & him,
but she shrugs & fades away
when the bitter drug weakens.

Free Maya Wu

Angry Maya Wu glared into his eyes
& said she was free — FUCKING FREE!
Fucking free to love other males & females.
Fucking free to be his friend & lover.
Fucking free to do anything she wanted,
but she didn't want to be owned
by him or any human being.
The foolish Great Basin boy nodded,
whispered, "Far out," but
he winced as the spike
pierced her vein
& the white powder
became her blood.

Shoshone Boots

Sweet, sexual, slightly mad
on "Black Beauties," the boys are
crashing at the Berkeley Provo house
near the ass-end of University Avenue
with wall to wall humans snoring
& it's past midnight & Doyle
is trying to get inside this little
Minnesota blonde's panties
when this big black wino stands
up & says, "I does the bangin'
around here," & arches tall &
pulls a blade from his suede boots
with cornball fringed tops.
Naatsi, unarmed, feels naked.
Doyle snorts and gets up
from a rumpled pile of blankets.
"Nice boots," says Doyle
& the huge black cat goes,
"Yeah, these is . . .
Shoshone boots!"

Ah come on now . . .
Shoshone boots?
Say what?

Naatsi starts giggling, thinking
of the *Newe* boys back home
& how one day he'd tell them

he met one of their relatives.
Then Doyle stands taller & barks,
"Soul brother, tonight ME
does the bangin' around here,"
& the brother's eyes
roll like a slot machine
& he slips his knife back
into his Shoshone boots.
Doyle has wild Irish eyes
that could make steel limp.

Twenty minutes later,
Doyle is pumping
away & *Naatsi* whispers,
"ME does the bangin'?"
& Doyle begins to snort
& laugh so hard he falls
out of the saddle
so . . . in gleeful ignorance
Naatsi hops aboard
& takes sloppy seconds
with pride & gratitude
from the little
Minnesota blonde.

"ME does the bangin',"
he tells her.

Maya Wu's Works

She rolls her eyes
in silence & smiles.
Her merchant parents
in exasperated harangue
across The City on the phone
can't figure her out.
They are not alone.
Maya Wu's body
makes him drool
but her works on the sink
stun his desert heart silent.

Indian Girls on Polk Street

Summer in The City
& he was celebrating
his twenty-first birthday
with these Indian girls
in the bar on Polk Street.
They said they were Arapaho
or maybe Assiniboine, hard to tell
they talked with such deep voices.
When he went to take a leak,
both came into the head
& one splashed cold water
over her face & took a quick shave.
"*Enit?*" he asked.
"*Enit,*" she answered.
"Holy shit," *Naatsi* gasped
when the other one lifted
her dress & stood next to him
at the urinal & shook
her thick eight-inch stinger.
Freaked out & in a hurry to
split the scene, *Naatsi* caught
his own ample flesh in his zipper.
He shrieked, then beat feet
far from those crazed bitches
& their chorus of Indian giggles.

Paiute Girl

She was there but he never saw her.
His mom's letter said she died
in a bathtub from a heroin overdose
in a place not far from where
he was crashing with Maya.
His mind was blown.
His own desert kin, *Numu,*
people of the pinenut & buckberry,
dying on the streets of San Francisco.
He promised himself he wouldn't be next
& wrote his mom he was working
& going to a church
& in the fall he'd go back to school
& he did . . . almost ten years later
& *the rat's tail fell off.*

Psychedelic Buddha

hip'pie, *n.* any of the young people of the 1960's who, in their
alienation from conventional society, have turned variously to
mysticism, psychedelic drugs, communal living, experimental
arts, etc. [Slang.]
— *Webster's New Unabridged Dictionary*

After twenty trips
acid became a roller coaster
filled with puking red-eyed monkeys
but Timothy–Goofball–Leary, the first trip
Naatsi took was with Maya . . . Man!
He heard cars breathing, panting,
whispering, "Oh, my aching crankshaft"
& other automotive atrocities.
He beamed over to Maya's pad
& their searing flesh melted
into a blue Godhead of flame.
They had one pair of lungs
& one huge sexual organ that shot
off sparks every time they touched it.
It cooed to them & became their Buddha.
Maya said it spoke Cantonese
but it sounded like Nevada
moon-howling to him.

Comanche

Crazy word subtractions
& additions won't bring back
the honor, the noble past
of the ancients & nothing can bring
back his Comanche friend
except a brief crack
in the eyeball of time. *Naatsi*
is dreaming-drunk & mumbling . . .

It's San Francisco 1967
& it might be Hell
though it looks like Heaven.
Damn that Comanche . . . who
dragged him down ditches
of red-eyed glee.
Damn that Comanche . . . whose
Indian weakness with whiskey
& dope created the sickness
of savage art & who painted
the ghosts of his dirt-poor mind
& sent them scurrying to no future.

What can *Naatsi* say now?
What could he do then?
He's forgotten much but remembers
Comanche in that Tenderloin roach
hotel where he cooked them
a can of Campbell's noodle soup

on a hotplate the Welfare bought
when they freed Comanche
from the human zoo.

The clouds of the 60's turned
bilious gray & green & sad
Pacific rains swept in.
They blackfaced noon as black as
the back of a smack cooking spoon.
When thunder cherry-bombed the room,
Naatsi countered nature's gloom by
rolling some righteous weed
he'd just scored.

The storm's upset stomach raged.
They fired back a more subtle gauge.
They lost the battle, but who kept score?
They matched broadsides flash for flash,
giggled & waited for both storms to crash.

Weeks later Comanche razored his wrists
& now decades later *Naatsi* admits
he's still somewhat pissed
at his brother that sweet
drawling Okie
who took the easy way out.

Chasing a Ghost

For Janet

I.

The mad moon had paid
its price & was bloodless
& paler than rice
& Maya was AWOL.
Washed out by a nagging head
cold, *Naatsi* was angered
by the bold sweep
of the Tactical Squad
& their recent wordless
hassling of the street freaks'
stoned yet peaceful coping.

Through the window,
he was startled to see
a dark Coyote girl loping
through the Fell Street mist
so he grabbed some joints
& quickly pissed then ran
out beyond the guilt of lust
conquering conscience to
do what he must.

Coyotes need kin to sniff
when they're trapped in gray
valleys of smog & steel
with citified two-legged
beasts.

II.

When he reached the street
she'd completely vanished
& he heard an eagle scream
from his mind's blurred
sky & something ancient
deep inside his hard
young heart throbbed
an unearthly ache
for blood abandoned.

It wasn't just Coyote girls
that he missed, but the wild-ass
essence of ancestral soil.
So, desert ghosts *had* followed
him across the high Sierras
& into this weird new world.
Desert ghosts, with deadly
dry desert humor.

The Boy Distinctly Remembers

They say if you can remember the 60's
then you weren't there, but he distinctly
remembers him & Doyle late
one night stuck on Fillmore Street
coming back from a Dead concert
& Doyle's raving at the luminous
pimps & the languid junkies
who scatter randomly
into chromium & steel scarabs
& Doyle, who could unconsciously
wax poetic, says something like:

They's on their way to
the pyramids not knowing
of Nefertiti or the mummy
of mammy inside their balls
begging to be eaten with
barbecue sauce—

Heart chilled by the angry whiteness
of his friend, *Naatsi*
hushes him lest they
get shanked.

Girl from Outer Space

She was sitting naked
& he leered & thoughtsang:

O Medusa oblongata.
Lordy, Lordy, oxen free!
O sad-ass lady
of the low, lowlands . . .

She was a deranged incarnation
of the beautiful terror of
the street they called Love.
"Total freakout—acid burned
out her brain," they whispered
at his connection's Cole Street pad
where he'd gone to see if maybe
they'd front him some lids.
Grinning & drooling,
she crouched on a couch
& flashed her beaver
—dared *Naatsi* to park
his car in her garage, so
he did & damn she was fine
but then she got diarrhea
of the mouth & mind.

He was really thinking
she looked like she might
have had Indian blood

dancing through her veins
until she dervished, sweating
around the room screeching she
was from the planet Zyronika.

ZYRONIKA??!!

He giggled, then grimaced
& quickly got dressed.
Gave her a handshake
& split into nightfall.
Among the stars, something
brilliant orange-yellow flashed.
It could've been Zyronika
exploding in sadness.
It could've been the Great Spirit
burning the shack set
aside for his soul.
He crossed his wet eyes
& howled a blue howl
as sad as his cold
heart could stomach.

Glossolalia

I.

It's the Mexican Day
of the Dead & Doyle & he
are happily hypnotizing
San Francisco from Coit Tower.
After sampling a dime bag
of Acapulco Gold, the
desert dropout from
the playas & black rock
of dusty northern Nevada
listens to his pal pray.
Doyle says:

Hooooooooooooooooooooooo
ray. Hoooo rah.
Rye chussssss.
Mary. Juan. Ahhhh!

O dear ghosts of Neruda's nuts,
Naatsi writes it down & will puzzle
over that scrap of paper
thirty years later.

II.

There's another scrap of paper,
a napkin from a bar, a memento.
Most of his memories of the Haight
will blur & he has very few photos

to prove he was there. *Maybe it was
all a mirage.* A recent poll says one
in five Americans do not believe
the Holocaust ever happened.
But he saved the napkin with
handwriting from Doyle.

It's January 18, 1967; it's raining.
Doyle is back from hustling for
dope money in a gay bar off Market.
He reads *Naatsi* crazed words he
transcribed onto a cocktail
napkin after overhearing
a drunk black dyke say:

*My girl got a little pussy
& it taste good too.
She's an Indian girl &
she ain't gotta be American
if she don't wanna be.*

Doyle thought the words hilarious.
He wrote them down as a joke
to tease his friend, simply because
Indian pussy was mentioned.
Naatsi was high on hash when
Doyle read the words to him.
Ain't gotta be American . . .
That sounded good to *Naatsi.*
Always has.
Always will.

At the Freight Yards

The ghost of Jesse James cornholes Doyle
in fading Richmond freight yard dusk.
Imagined train time harmonicas
warble sadder than Dylan
& warn the majestic iron horse
of their stand upon the tracks.
Outlaw Doyle wants to hobo back east
but his invisible six-shooters
can't stop the dark tons of steel.
Whispers of death roar
through the California night.
The cast-iron catatonic
grumbles past & drowns out
the chirps of citified crickets.
The Southern Pacific beacon frown
lights diesel smoke inside their brains
& they hail the black caboose
& fail & hitch back to The City
& follow their shadows
back up the crazed slopes
to the heights of the Haight
& beyond.

Blind Hippie Girl

It's dusk & the drone of blue fog
oozes over San Francisco.
Blinking jets trail off into history.
Naatsi sits yoga-style on
a bench in Golden Gate Park & tells
a sightless angel all he can see.
Through his mask of duty, he itemizes
an unwashed freak's eyes, dilated
& demonic, far out of sync with lips
whispering, "Lids, acid, hash . . .
spare change?"

For her, he wordpaints bell-bottom
freaks with love beads & dirty feet
stonedancing some nature strut
straight out of Stonehenge.
In return, she promises to tell him
how the morning sun sounds.
She runs her hand from his thigh
to his glistening fangs & rips off
his mask of duty & soon
they are blind-thrashing
getting groin-wet
on green grass.

Mescaline

In a lonely room
in a stranger's house
he stares into the mirror
& his face explodes
into a kaleidoscope of flames.
He whirls to the window
& frantically lifts it open
to let the cold air strangle the fire.
He hears the desperate zipping traffic.
The December breeze stabs his heart.
Swirling winter fog blows
his dandelion brain up to the stars
where it recollects & whispers
to a thousand reservation
& small town dreamers:

Stay away from The City.
It's all an illusion. A deadly illusion.
A sleight of hand to mouth to brain
that will cripple & mindfuck your soul.

Lord, it's Christmas 1968
& there's not a whole lot of merry
in the foul manger called "The Haight."

The Whipping Snake Dream

Drunk, he was crying in his beer because
Maya Wu was out trekking her junkie trail
so he dropped some Mind Detergent.
A dumb-ass mistake to trip drunk & down.
A sure-fire recipe for a bummer.

Four hours of horrors followed
& then he felt the blessed touch of sleep.
But dopehead drunks don't have sober dreams.
So, he pretended he was back on Indian land
& dreamed of a red whipping snake.
It was rubber & metal & spitting suds.
It was . . .
a shattered shot glass covered with blood.
A poverty-addled baby's wail.
A moaning mountain of broken arrows.
A car wreck cousin's cheap wooden casket.
An endless highway of roadkilled coyotes.
It was two million red-souled people writing
the word FAILURE on one tiny chalkboard.
It was rubber & metal & spitting suds.

He pretended he was back
on Indian land & dreamed
of a red whipping snake
but awoke to moaning walls,
rapid pulse & no toilet paper.
He awoke on the floor eye to eye

with an ancient orange
somehow fallen under the bed
& turned green & harder
than Jesus before Mary Magdalene.
Yes, brothers, he pretended he was back
on Indian land but was staunchly sober
when he woke to a rock-hardgreen orange.
He scoped it as if it were a space alien.
Perhaps the orange was the child
of the red whipping snake
of rubber & metal & spitting suds.
He cradled it & held it to his sober ear.
It whispered songs so sacred
that they became profane.
It told him to eat spirit-snake semen
& drink hot dreamblood from the holy
piss & vinegar fountain of youth.
He did & radiated flame.
Was this the end?
If so, his only wish was to write
his own obituary & say he died
smiling & gloriously drunk
& that his smile
was faintly hued with
the sunset of Maya's lipstick.

Garish red, harsh & loving lipstick.

The Boy Runs into Maya Wu
At Morningstar Commune

Late at night camping
out the boy was floating
stoned on a green cloud
happily humming wind songs.
His lips twisted kisses at hairy,
smiling stars when silent crickets
signaled someone coming.
Holy magnitude of muted bugs!
His solitude of songs was shattered soundly.
The blacktop snake stretching between
the fields bloomed a night flower.
O sweet bones formed from simple chop suey!
It *was* Maya & she appeared in
a blue aura & calmed his reefer madness.
They both threw peace signs & she ran
to him, smelling of woodsmoke,
young & alive, young & alive
& so in love with her half-breed stud.

Pacific Highway: 1968

His tears on the beach sand
do not spell a haunting
song of lost America.
There is no stolen
country of his dreams.
Nobody has played the
game of "Indian giving."
Nobody played perversion
on his youngman ears &
nobody provided a hiding place
for his future fears to gestate
before they burst out of his penis
like hordes of black widows.
Naatsi is happy with his Asian
junkie on a purple foaming beach
in a pink midnight year.
Lebanese kef creates a distant
tinkle of piano blues. Maya is
naked beneath a blue wool cape.
Slow Pacific fog trips onto land.
He prays that when he's an old man
dying, he will remember this
tumescent & wondrous night.

Mission Street Crash Pad

The barrio bells woke him.
Soft Chicano babble wafted
up to his groggy eardrums
breeding visions of *conquistadores,*
crosses soaked in flaming crimson,
Coronado, galleons, even Zorro
crossed his mind, moonlight
on the hacienda, casks of
sweet Castilian wine.

But then he walked into the kitchen
& there before the sun struck noon
his China Girl & some Aztec junkie
were cooking breakfast
in a spoon & humming
a lame-ass Simon
& Garfunkel tune.

San Francisco: 1969

Babylon is fallen, is fallen, that great city.
—REVELATIONS 14:8

The heartless city by the bay is
swiftly approaching a new decade.
In some cornball straight
universe Tony Bennett was crooning
his cornhole ballad but now viral
Hell had arrived in paradise:
the speed freaks, bikers, the ex-cons,
the pimps, greedy dope dealers,
the fear the CIA was tainting drugs,
the rip-off artists, narcs in the bushes
& all the lost & longing white
Indians brought him down.

So, he . . .
swallowed some Blue Cheer,
hoping to wash away the goblins
& after he started tripping saw Maya
strung out on skag levitating toward
Stanyan Street with some
greasy-dick Fillmore pimp.
She smiled at *Naatsi,* but he
couldn't, wouldn't smile at her.

Life is sacred, yet nothing is sacred.
Red eyes hid behind her dark glasses.
She looked like a sluttish vampire.
Her dead fish lips smiled faintly
at him & he didn't know

whether to shit or go blind.
His heart felt drained of blood.
His hands twitched & his balls
quivered, shriveled in his jeans.
He didn't know whether to puke or cry.
He shook his head & turned his back.
He turned his back & walked away.
Hours later, centuries, light-years later,
coming down, he found Doyle
& they made a decision to hitch east
& split from the Haight.
The love had died.
From this spot onward,
the nation is dying . . .
Sparkling psychedelic snakes
worm-danced up from the earth
& spritzed through the air.
Iridescent maggots were everywhere.
Everywhere, the love,
the love, the fucking
LOVE
had
DIED.

His Unsent Letter to Maya Wu

My Dear Maya,
Was it only a junkie's dream that
made you see America as nothing
more than a nation of greedy little
men seated behind grimy windows,
praying for their missing souls?
Off-key & bloodless, our love words
flew like pink midnight pigeons
dilating from sockets of concrete
making us run from alley to
alley to avoid being hit.

O Maya, is it a dream now when
you appear like a white owl sprung
from a mist of ghost breath & our past
swaggers in like a warm SF night?
Those patchouli years *were* losing
magic when we caged our hearts
inside one of those liquid
dimestore snowflake orbs.
I sweated acid our last night together.
I shook until a brain-blizzard swirled.
You were probably having nightmares
about the "got to make it" dreams
of your Chinatown parents
when I climbed up the chimney
& flew home & then later flew
galaxies away from my homeland too.

Now scrolling through this dusk
of my youthful mind's mush, I recall
numerous times I kissed the bright air
masking the musk of some aging lush.
They gave what you gave—I gave them
green. I came & they went.
What was in between was only
your shadow mad dancing
through my puppy-love dreams.
It's been more than three decades
since I flew far from you. We were
verdant eagles of opposite poles.
Sixteen years have passed since
your last postcard came.
Sixteen halved by two is eight.
China Girl, eight halved by two
was never four for us.
Three was the number of intrusion.
The infidel white powder
was our destroyer. Darling, it's 1999.
Cruel & thirsty years have passed.
Eating alone in this rez mini-mart,
I greet my weary false-flamed burgers.
The ennui of my own flesh allows no
pity for the anemic kiss of fire tonight.
Damn, it's so deadly dreary to mope
but darling, it *was* you & me,
sitting in a tree—K I SS ING.
China Girl, the memory of your eyes
forms these words & my ears try to
make sense of the insidious lines
in the age-tracked face frowning

upon my hallway mirror . . .
I can no longer hear my soul.
I think all men must sing this song.

That night we stood in the cave of the soul
barbecue on Haight Street an uncertain
weariness moved our hands to touch.
The room was cloud-filled with meat smoke.
A lance of light hurtled through
the darkness & slashed the snakeskins
of our years & we promised to be stoned
fools forever, to glue groins forever,
whatever forever means to the young.

Ancient Acid Flashes Back

I.

September in one of the jungle war years.
Doyle & *Naatsi* were hitching east
with no money in their pockets
but they had new pea coats
from some sailor boys who traded
for lids & their pockets were filled
with packs of peanuts & two new blues
harps & somewhere in the interior
of California they got stranded near
a highway sign that said:
APPLE VALLEY, HOME OF ROY ROGERS' RANCH.
Doyle chortled & pulled out the last joint
of gold & they toked up, got whacked
& played their harps, first loony
"Sad-Eyed Lady of the Lowlands"
& then "Happy Trails" & later coming
down with no rides on the horizon
Doyle screamed, "Trigger, darling . . .
I know Roy's porking you.
& you love it!"

II.

Things got bad somewhere in Texas on Route 66.
It was raining, cold. Hungry & sleepless, they
huddled in a culvert under the highway
where they built a small fire & chewed
some prairie grass & shared the last cigarette.

Doyle said *Naatsi* "niggerlipped it!"
Naatsi said, "Shove your white arrogance!"
so Doyle got pissed & they pushed each
other down into the mud, fists flailing,
the dark soil of Sam Houston
& Lee Harvey Oswald
browncaking their blue pea coats.
They got up, eyes shooting flames
& Doyle headed east & *Naatsi*
skulked toward the west of his birth.
Fifteen minutes in the rain
brought Doyle back to him.
They both apologized & Doyle confessed
he had a tab of Owsley stashed
so they split it & went back
under the culvert which melted
& sang to them for hours, years.
It sang songs of concrete.
It sang of America's sweet possibilities.

Naatsi really thought he'd forgotten
those tunes & times
but ancient acid is flashing back.
Thirty years later, he hears sitars
& thinks he smells distant patchouli.

April 24, 1971

It's his birthday
& he's twenty-five
on the lawn in DC
near the Lincoln Memorial
getting a wicked hand job
from some white girl he just met.
There's lots of people around.
Maybe 500,000 humans.
They're protesting Vietnam.
FIVE HUNDRED THOUSAND
American sexual organs!
He shoots his load shortly
before the tear gas cannons
begin their first bombardment.
Maybe the revolution has started
but *Naatsi* no longer cares.
The 60's are over &
he's tired of scenes.
The 60's are over
& the future looks
mind-dead & televised,
grim, greedy & goofy.

Requiems for Dead Dreams

I.
Smoke & candles, incense & rock.
Bolts of Delhi cloth on the windows.
Outside, America was murdering freedom.

II.
He was just a desert boy. It was the fragrance
of the eucalyptus trees on Fell & Oak that stoned
him more than any weed ever could.

III.
Was it all a dream? The 1999 Rand McNally
Road Atlas does not even show Haight Street,
the yellow brick road that briefly goosed the USA.

IV.
This cannibal nation severed the index
finger of his peace sign. A solitary requiem,
his middle finger remains standing.

Vanilla Fudge

"Okay," *Naatsi* said
to the long-distance
caller & rolled his eyes.
"Maybe Bill Clinton
was there somewhere in the 60's
smoking a joint but not inhaling."
"Yeah," he said & closed his eyes.
"I can almost flash on young Bubba,
standing off in the corner
with some plastic
college daytrippers
pretending to toke
off that joint
so he wouldn't have
to spring that lame
cracker accent &
deep deep down
wishing he could dig
Jimi Hendrix as well
as he dug Vanilla Fudge
& hope-hope-hoping
he could just score
him some head."

Trees, Rush Limbaugh, & the Failed Exorcism of Maya Wu's Ghost

April 1999.
He was dreamflashing on
the eucalyptus trees in Golden
Gate Park thirty years ago
but then he snapped out of it.
He exorcised the demons.

It is spring on the Great Plains
but the endless winter made sure
his poplars were dead to the roots
& his old elms have finally refused
to bud another year for the beetles.
Dog pee has killed his young cedars.
Damned crackhead Sioux chopped down
his two blue spruces at Christmas.

His lilacs are verdant & rampant
with weak-scented flowers but
Naatsi doubts they'll support a noose.
Some days he wants to call Dr. Kevorkian
because he's contracted some deep
form of madness that allows
Rush Limbaugh to make sense to him.

Sometimes he just doesn't know . . .
He's wearied & worried too often —
a million things to fret about.
On *Good Morning America* he sees

a florid, semi-puffy Bill Clinton
jogging & sweating out
the Big Macs & dodging questions
about whether he has a soul or not.
Clinton's nose looks red & bulbous.
Eight years in office made him look old.
Naatsi himself is as old as Clinton . . .
No, no, he's younger than Bubba!

Okay, *yes,* he *was* dreamflashing
on the eucalyptus
trees in Golden Gate Park
thirty years ago, but he
figured he'd snapped out of it.

Okay, he *was* standing
under those fragrant trees
& Maya Wu *was* at his side.
The earth shimmered through
the cosmos while they laughed
& sang, so stoned on the bittersweet
joyride of life & on mad, mad
love & destruction.

It Was a World of Ideas

It was a world of ideas
& ineffable human kindness
but young *Naatsi*
was a mandog of flesh.
His memory will not scrawl
the yellow-robed Hare Krishnas
goofy-ass drumming & bouncing
down the street called Love
even though he still romanticizes his days
among the dealers & the panhandlers
& he still can taste the freedom
found in the black cornsilk
of Maya's sweet groin.

It was a world of ideas
& ineffable human kindness
that thirty years later has caused
him to bawl, *Maya, where you at?*
one sober moon-bright night
with snow falling bleakly
onto the Badlands.

Where the hell
are you, love, & where
the holy hell am I?

Postscript: A Case Study

Always been an outsider, a half-breed
Indian relegated by self & others to margins
but in the Haight *Naatsi* saw the living borderlands
of American life—a homeland for outsiders,
a skidrow church of the mind choreographed
with anthems of acid rock & shaded
with dread, a living paranoia that he was doing
something so deathly wrong by breaking rules
that the so-called ESTABLISHMENT
would eventually catch on & erase him.
He wasn't a dumb kid, so he feared America.
In '64 he graduated from a small, dusty
high school in the same valley where the Paiute
prophet Wovoka started the "Ghost Dance."
He grew up dirt-poor, the eldest in a flock
of twelve half-breed Paiute kids & he was
the first in the family ever to try college.

In '65, *Naatsi* went through "Hell Week"
with the *ATΩ* fraternity at the U. in Reno.
Their national charter forbade Indians,
Jews, Blacks & Asians, but a handful
of Indians were allowed in. In the spring
of that year, with some of his new "brothers,"
he drove down to Berkeley for a conference
& they all got puking drunk & rowdy.
Dressed in madras shirts, white Levi's
& low-cut black Converse tennies

they slouched out into the strange
California night looking for beatnik
(or maybe Mario Savio's) ass to kick.
But there were so many scary-looking
weirdos along Telegraph Avenue that they
slinked back to the frat house with their tails
between their legs—knew better than to start
a rumble against superior odds . . .
He flunked out the second semester & stayed
out for another imitating a laborer
in a copper mine at Yerington, Nevada.
Then he returned to the U. & re-flunked out.
Figured college was for guzzling beer &
chasing the bearded clam. Blame it on karma,
but a year & a half after he first visited Berkeley,
he found himself there again, but the Great Spirit
had recast him as a stoned-out, hairy weirdo.
He'd become a "freak," one of those bizarre
miscreants he'd despised on first sight—hanging
out on Telegraph Avenue & evading the terminal
rot of greendeath Asia. Maybe he just wanted
the hell out of the rural time warp of redneck
backwater Nevada. Whatever—*Naatsi* had
enlisted in a cosmic army searching for
the meaning of life, so from Berkeley he
migrated across the Bay Bridge
to the Haight-Ashbury & spent several
years with "white Indians" camped there
whose illusory hope for a better world
has lasted inside him for thirty years.
Sure, the Haight *was* awash with chemicals
& too many people believed in a loony

& self-destructive experimentation with drugs
but dope *was* the joking God they believed in.

Today when *Naatsi* eyeballs the crack epidemic,
the AIDS plague, the drug gangs, the welfare state,
& the general incompetence & aimlessness
of this lost nation, he's haunted by the feeling
that they failed—that they lived a lie, or at best,
a shallow & indulgent escapism.
They tried to tame the manic,
anal-retentive beast that America was,
but they only wounded & maddened it
& it's gnawing now on your
fucking front door!

About the Author

A half-breed Indian, Adrian C. Louis was born and raised in Nevada and is an enrolled member of the Lovelock Paiute Tribe. From 1984 to 1998, he taught at Oglala Lakota College on the Pine Ridge Reservation of South Dakota. Prior to this, Louis edited four Native newspapers, including a stint as managing editor of *Indian Country Today*. He currently teaches at Southwest State University in Minnesota.

Louis has written eight books of poems including *Fire Water World,* winner of the 1989 Poetry Center Award from San Francisco State University. He has also written two works of fiction: *Skins,* a novel, and *Wild Indians & Other Creatures,* short stories.

Adrian C. Louis has won various writing awards including a Pushcart Prize and fellowships from the Bush Foundation, the National Endowment for the Arts, and the Lila Wallace–Reader's Digest Foundation. In 1999 he was elected to the Nevada Writers' Hall of Fame.